I'VE BEEN MEANING TO TELL YOU

I'VE BEEN MEANING TO TELL YOU

DAVID CHARIANDY

BLOOMSBURY PUBLISHING

NEW YORK · LONDON · OXFORD · NEW DELHI · SYDNEY

BLOOMSBURY PUBLISHING
Bloomsbury Publishing Inc.
1385 Broadway, New York, NY 10018, USA

BLOOMSBURY, BLOOMSBURY PUBLISHING, and the Diana logo are trademarks
of Bloomsbury Publishing Plc

First published in 2018 in Canada by McClelland & Stewart
First published in the United States 2019

ISBN: HB: 978-1-63557-287-2; eBook: 978-1-63557-288-9

Library of Congress Cataloging-in-Publication Data is available

A catalogue record for this book is available from the British Library

2 4 6 8 10 9 7 5 3 1

Typeset by Integra Software Services Pvt. Ltd.
Printed and bound in the U.S.A. By Berryville Graphics Inc., Berryville, Virginia

To find out more about our authors and books visit www.bloomsbury.com
and sign up for our newsletters.

Bloomsbury books may be purchased for business or promotional use. For
information on bulk purchases please contact Macmillan Corporate and
Premium Sales Department at specialmarkets@macmillan.com.

THE OCCASION

Once, when you were three, we made a trip out for lunch. We bussed west in our city, to one of those grocery-store buffets serving the type of food my own parents would scorn. Those overpriced organics laid out thinly in brushed-steel trays, the glass sneeze guard just high enough for you, dearest daughter, to dip your head beneath it in assessing, suspiciously, the "browned rice" and "free-range carrots." And in that moment, I could imagine myself a father long beyond the grip of history, and now caring for his loved one through kale and quinoa and a soda boasting "real cane sugar."

But we're both dessert people, a soda won't cut it, and so we shared a big piece of chocolate cake. "It's good for you," you giggled. "Chocolate cake is very, very good for you." You squirmed away as I tried to wipe your mouth, laughing at all of my best efforts. It was an ordinary moment. And an ordinary thirst was brought on by the thick sweet of the cake, and so I stood and moved towards the nearby tap to get us both a glass of water, encountering a woman on her way to do the same thing. She was nicely dressed, a light summer cream suit, little makeup, tasteful. We reached the tap at roughly the same time. I hesitated out of a politeness, and this very gesture seemed only to irritate her. She shouldered herself in front of me, and when filling her glass of water, she half turned to explain, "I was born here. I belong here."

Her voice was loud. She meant to be overheard, to provoke agreement, maybe, although the people lunching around us reacted only by focusing harder upon their own bowls and plates. And you, my daughter, sitting closest, didn't understand, or else you didn't even hear. You were still in a moment of joy, your own laughter filling your ears, the dark frosting between your teeth, and so I decided. I waited patiently to fill our glasses. I walked carefully back to you, never spilling a drop. I sat. I might have tried to match your smile. I might have attempted once more to wipe your mouth, or asked you to take a sip of water to prevent dehydration, the latest foolish fear of parents like me. I don't remember. I sometimes find myself in this state during the course of an ordinary day. I was lost in thought and quiet, even after I caught your hand waving before my eyes. Your face now cross and confused. "Hey," you asked, "what happened?"

Today, a decade later, we still find occasions to go out, just the two of us, although I know that what you sometimes need is space. Under your direction, we fixed up a room for you in the basement, painting the walls a specific shade of seafoam, adding better lighting, a twin bed with your first real mattress, and a door that, when the mood requires, can softly close. Against your brother, with whom you used to share a room. Against your parents. Against an intruding and perplexing world. "It's normal for a girl at this age, this desire for privacy," some parents have told me, although I've spent my whole life never taking for granted what is "normal." You're thirteen years old, this much is certain. This is your last year of elementary school, and this is also the 150th anniversary of the country in which we both were born.

You are a girl, but this again offers me little I can take for granted. When very small, you decided that you hated pink and also princesses, even the ostensibly modern ones with their conventional prettiness now

3

super-powered. You refused to wear a dress, arguing it was a nuisance when cartwheeling and somersaulting. And today you remain a blur of motion, pure fierceness at the dojo where you train and spar with adults who tower over you. Recently, when we were in the kitchen together, a news story came on the radio about a man whose criminal charge was reduced from murder to manslaughter. "Manslaughter?" you said. "But that sounds way worse than murder!" I tried to explain that manslaughter involved someone being killed, but without conscious intent. "Suppose a man tried to assault you," I began, "but in defending yourself you punched him so hard that he fell back and cracked his head on the pavement and died. You weren't deliberately trying to kill him, right? But that might be considered manslaughter even though it was an accident." You thought for a moment, nodding. "I see your point," you said. "That would be awful. But I wouldn't exactly call my punch an accident. I would call it forceful and correct technique."

I've told this story to other parents, receiving smiles both real and markedly awkward, sometimes the laugh one gives when something is cute, but I know I've never been successful in conveying its true meaning for me. When I was a boy your age, I'm not sure if I could have expressed so easily my right to defend my body from harm—not only my right to physical safety but my right to acknowledge and push back against denigration of any sort, great or small. To witness you, my daughter, so physically confident in your body, is to be awed and also to wonder at how much your childhood differs from mine. Certainly you possess a worldliness that was unthinkable to me at your age. You've had the opportunity to visit Europe and countries throughout North America, and you wish to see much more; you seem to have little of the anxiety I often feel about crossing borders and encountering new people in different spaces. You go to a French immersion school, not only because your mother, raised and educated in Quebec, wished this for you, but because I too hoped that you would not be trapped, as I am, in a single language. And yet the irony is that your very success has turned me into the imaginary immigrant parent I never thought I would be, proud of his daughter's accomplishments in school, yet unable to help her with even her grade seven homework.

Maybe the differences between our childhoods are but a version of those that exist between many parents and children. My own parents, your beloved grandparents, were not imaginary immigrant parents but real and specific ones, Black and South Asian people who journeyed to this country more than half a century ago, who worked lifelong as a minder of children and a factory labourer. They experienced many indignities and deep body aches, sacrifices and shortages, but they worked hard and they managed to raise a writer who is also a professor of literature, a fact of which they are proud but also, at times, perplexed. They do not understand every-thing about me, but I'm sure they believe, for good reason, that they have provided a better life for their son, and that many if not all the challenges they once experienced no longer affect me.

At times, I'm tempted to imagine the same of you. You go to a school that displays posters in the hallways abstractly warning against discrimination and bullying, while celebrating inclusion and diversity. You once decided to do a project on the Underground Railroad, and you were supported in this by your teacher. You have been introduced to books by particular authors and in particular voices that I was never introduced to in either primary or secondary school: *The Diary of Anne Frank*, *I Am Malala*, *The Book of Negroes*. You show me YouTube videos posted by a Brown girl who, like me, grew up in Scarborough, someone who seems to have no fear in airing to the world her ideas, her opinions, even her everyday silliness. She is, you solemnly inform me, a girl who experienced rough moments and serious doubts, but who overcame them and learned courage and now advises others how likewise to be a "Bawse."

There is a song entitled "On Children" by the group Sweet Honey in the Rock. It's not a song you'd ordinar-ily come across, I know. It's based on a poem by Kahlil Gibran, who was born in what we now call Lebanon and who migrated to the United States. Long after his death the words of his poem have been animated with new feeling and meaning by the Black women singing them. "Your children are not your children," Sweet Honey in the Rock sing. "They are the sons and daughters of Life's longing for itself. They come through you but they are not from you, and though they are with you, they belong not to you. . . . For their souls dwell in a place of tomorrow, which you cannot visit, not even in your dreams." It is a beautiful and very humbling song for any father who imagines that he might pass on to his daughter wisdom born of experience, of a personal or familial past.

But I find myself wondering just when a child begins to dwell in that place of tomorrow. I wonder, most often, about your life in the place of today, and what you have already seen and heard, have already understood and been made to feel. I wonder if there are moments, despite your tough postures, when you have felt neither confident nor safe. I wonder about the persistent messages sent to girls in the news, in movies, in language and image, and in the rhetoric of politics and business, especially girls who share your ancestry but who have not had your special opportunities.

I wonder about the electronic "tomorrow" that you are already navigating in your basement room, when at night you peer into a screen and the world casts its lurid energies upon your brown face.

★

On the day of your thirteenth birthday, we celebrated, at your request, with just close family. Present on that day were your grandmother and grandfather, people who now, in their eighties, count among the greatest triumphs in their life the possibility to be here with you, to cook a meal for you, to cup in their hands your face, to touch your living flesh. Present too, of course, was your mother, a woman who would be the first to admit that she grew up with great privilege but who has dedicated her life to learning what it means to live ethically as a white settler upon Indigenous land. Present too was your younger brother, who is dreamy and kind and brilliant, who admires and loves you more than anybody in the world, and whom you largely tolerate and also love deeply. We are a family of different generations, different upbringings, different backgrounds and races—diverse in ways no half-hearted policy or opportunistic advertisement campaign can ever truly represent, and brought together in the celebration of your birth. But in that moment, we were also made to experience "history." For your thirteenth birthday was but a couple of days before the inauguration of a new American president.

I am rarely surprised by the language and outcomes of electoral politics. But the campaign that resulted in the 2017 inauguration was the first you followed in any detail, and for this I apologize. I'm sorry for both the subtle and overt denigration of women, the casual vitriol against refugees, Mexicans, and Muslims. I apologize, most of all, that at your thirteenth birthday party, the conversation around the table turned away from the celebration of your life to the spectacle of adult cynicism and idiocy. Your brother asked repeatedly if bullies should be allowed to win. Your mother spoke about the upcoming protest marches, about an "un-auguration" ceremony planned by a friend. Your grandfather had strong words, but your grandmother remained quiet, perhaps trying to stay in the celebration of you. And in that coronation of yet another spoiled and loudly boastful man who sought to close borders and "take our country back" at the expense of the hard-working and vulnerable, I wanted suddenly to tell you the quieter story of your grandparents, a story of migration and struggle and also of love between races taught to distrust one another.

To tell such a story would, of course, take time, and there was little of that. Two days later was the inauguration. And a week after that, we listened in shock to news of a travel ban on seven Muslim-majority countries and the suspension of refugee admissions. You were confused and worried. "Isn't this discrimination?" you asked. "Can it really happen?" They seemed rhetorical questions, or ones I didn't know quite how to answer, and after a short silence, you asked, in a softer voice, "Could it happen here?" For two hundred years, even before its official confederation, Canada has nursed the idea that it is fundamentally superior to its neighbour to the south. A sense that it is an exception in a world of intolerance, that when the language of bigotry and racism is whipped up elsewhere, it meets firm resistance at the 49th parallel. We both, already, know better than this. But in the fragility of that moment, when you asked if the travel ban could happen here, I said no, it could not, not today at least. But two days later, something else happened. A man apparently enthralled by the messages of Donald Trump and Marine Le Pen entered a mosque in Quebec City and executed six people who were at their prayers.

A day later, in the dark of the winter rains, we walked to a vigil at a nearby mosque. It is the oldest mosque in Vancouver, I learned only then, a quiet presence in a residential neighbourhood of mostly townhouses, low-rises, and apartment buildings, a modest but well-kept place of worship visited often by taxi drivers. The mosque had been the subject of a minor local news story when its members had decided to open its doors to provide emergency shelter and food for the homeless during a tough cold snap. The mosque had been the subject of another minor story a few months before that, when it was the target of arson, the fire sputtering out on the doorstep before it could cause major damage.

Approaching the vigil, we had noticed police cars and floodlights, and I felt your hand squeeze mine, or mine squeeze yours, but we both soon realized it was all for the mayor and other city representatives who were scheduled to show up. Your brother received a candle and did his best to shield it from the wet and wind. Prompted by some mysterious recognition of la Francophonie, a member of the mosque immediately began speaking in French to your mother, friendly small talk, your mother explained afterwards. There were speeches being made by people standing at the doors of the mosque, but there was no amplification system, and we weren't close enough to hear. A white city councillor started to cry before she finished speaking, and the man who seemed to be representing the mosque comforted her. He smiled throughout the ceremony. And I wondered if that smile said something about resilience, or about the mysterious power of faith, or perhaps about the masks that men of so many backgrounds feel compelled to wear in moments like these.

We are not Muslim. We do not face Islamophobia, the specificity and intensity of that bigotry, just as we are not Indigenous and so do not know that particular legacy of violence and survival. But the fact is that I require little imagination to understand what it feels like to be considered dispensable by the powerful within a country. To be viewed as unconnected to the fabric of Canadian society, or as a threat, singled out in lines and at borders, visibly targeted by those who are, in fact, the most secure. I do not *empathize* with victims of bigotry or racism; I *know* the feeling intimately and viscerally. Perhaps you feel this too. The next morning, you awoke with a mysterious illness. When I pressed, you wouldn't explain, and only after some coaxing, you whispered, "It's so bad. The world." I sat with you, trying to think of what to say, and was struck by the bad timing. One day later you would be leaving for a much-anticipated week-long exchange trip to a small town near Quebec City, the very site of the shooting. And what I feared most was that when I now needed to say more, to give some account of the world, and of our place in it, you would be so far away.

My own parents were cautious about revealing to me the story of their past. They found few words to give me about how their ancestors had come to be in the Americas, the horrors of slavery, the bitterness of indenture. They likewise spoke little about their upbringing in Trinidad, possibly because the traumas of that past were still so palpable, or else because, like many immigrants, they wished to imagine for themselves and for their children a new beginning. Even of their early life in Canada, they were careful what they revealed. My mother arrived here as a domestic worker in 1963, one of the few ways that a Black woman could bypass the immigration restrictions of the time. After a tough and lonely year, she sponsored my father, and together they experienced a country and a Toronto very different from the one that exists now. They found friends and allies: a Polish family who invited my parents to have their wedding reception in their home; a Scottish woman who shared food during shortages; a white Canadian man who helped them prove, for what it was worth, that apartments said to be rented were in fact very much available to "real" Canadians. But they faced many other incidents on their own. They were stared at and humiliated in public spaces; refused service in restaurants; told outright that they couldn't possibly expect the same pay for work as whites; and their home, when they could finally rent one, was pointedly vandalized.

"How did you know?" my mother and father both asked me, when one day I wrote about their experiences. Their faces held surprise, even something like fear, as if they had unintentionally leaked their secrets. But as you had reminded me over a slice of chocolate cake ten years ago, children always sense more than what their parents are willing to say. Children read stories in pauses and silences, from irritation and sadness, from the grief and fear behind brave faces. And children sometimes choose silence. A child will not always readily tell, for instance, how, growing up as a working-class Black boy in a white middle-class suburb, he comes to embody what is feared about a changing city and nation. He hesitates to convey his experiences because he wishes to be seen as tough. Or because it is the special nature of the hurt to feel shameful in reporting it. Or perhaps a child will not discuss the matter with his parents because, tragically, he has come to believe that it is not history but they who are to blame for the legacies of race.

You are thirteen, dearest daughter, some say a pivotal time in a person's life. A time from which the *real* you will emerge. People have said similar things about the historical moment in which we live. That this is a time when the push to justice may finally be achieved, or the work of generations turned back. I don't know about either. But I do still imagine this moment, dear daughter, as the occasion when I will tell you of my past. When I will speak to you as a father, someone who could never presume that his story could encompass your experiences, your body, your imagining of tomorrow, but someone who must tell his story all the same. "What happened?" I hear you asking, one more time. And this time I will find the courage to say.

THE TEST

Soon after you returned from Quebec, your mother and I had our bloodlines tested. Together, as a family, we opened a kit of glossy cardboard about the size and shape of a big hardcover book. The test promised "an unprecedented view into your deep ancestry," and it came from National Geographic, the publisher of a monthly magazine I remember from my childhood, mostly because it exposed me for the first time to pictures of naked people, though never individuals from North America or Europe. The test results would provide "a breakdown of your regional ancestry by percentage, going as far back as 200,000 years." It would produce "a rich report that reveals the anthropological story of your ancestors—where they lived and how they migrated." By mailing samples of our bodies to a distant lab of experts, your mother and I would learn the truths of our heredity and belonging. We would, in this way, be adding our "own chapter to the human story."

There are times, dearest daughter, when circumstances that appear to be ordinary to others strike me as difficult. When I know, at least dimly, why I feel the way I feel, but I cannot in the moment express it to others, cannot "use my words" as I've often asked you to do. All I remember is that on that day as we gathered around the dining room table to follow the instructions on the kit, a bad mood flooded over me. The checkerboard pictures of distinct human types on the enclosed pamphlet suddenly struck me as contrived and annoying. The scraping of my inner cheek for a sample of my DNA felt impossibly irritating; and even though I had been the one to buy the kit, I now grew suspicious, reasonably or not, about the prospect of submitting my body to anonymous men of science in the hope that they would tell me something pleasing about myself. There were little vials of liquid into which we were supposed to put our samples, probably to preserve them for the trip in the mail; and I am normally a very careful individual, but I somehow managed to topple the vial, its thin clear liquid seeping onto the table before us. "Careful," said your younger brother, pointing out the mishap.

You got upset, accusing me of ruining the test, ruining everything. I snapped back a bit too sharply and told you to settle down. You raised your voice still louder to tell *me* to settle down before turning your face away and blinking back tears. Your mother intervened. She reminded me that you had just returned from Quebec. That you had been sick for most of the visit, missing out on activities with your friends. That your French-speaking "twin," who had lived her whole life in a very small town, found it difficult to connect with you across the divides of language and culture. Your mother explained in a voice lowered just for me that you had felt removed from the family, and that this, right now, was supposed to be a moment of reconnection. "Can't you get a grip?" she whispered.

It was well into spring before the results of the test were available. You had set up an electronic notification system, and when it was time you summoned us all to the home computer. In the crazily fluent way of your generation, you began clicking and typing and mouse-pad-dragging your way through pages of information. Your mother understood herself to be Scottish on both sides, and she was hoping for evidence of something a bit more "interesting" in her background, but she discovered not only that she is entirely European but also that, even as a multigenerational settler Canadian, she has a significantly greater percentage of "Great Britain and Ireland" ancestry than the average person actually residing within Great Britain and Ireland. "More British than the British," I said, chuckling—perhaps a bit unwisely.

My own results were as expected. The two largest proportions of me are of "South Asian" and "Western and Central African" regional ancestry, although I apparently possess a sizable chunk of "Central Asian" ancestry, as well as proportions of "Polynesian," "Scandinavian," "Great Britain and Ireland," and "North African." Pointing out another percentage on the screen, I boasted to your mother that I had only about half as much Neanderthal DNA in me as the average human. "Surprising," she said.

You continued to navigate the screens of information, and we discovered that I am very distantly related to certain "famous historical geniuses": Abraham Lincoln, Charles Darwin, Maria Theresa, Copernicus, and Petrarch. I began to experience that complicated feeling that sometimes arrives when you and I are watching a popular movie or television show. We'll be enjoying the story and the sheer glitz and polish of the production, but I will also be noticing the complexion of the actors and who gets to play particular roles, and

I will wish to point this out but not want to ruin the fun. You clicked again, and we looked at the "heat maps" of my ancestry, my "paternal line" lighting up in orange and yellow almost all of Asia and Europe, and my "maternal line" lighting with concentrated colour only the continent of Africa. I remember feeling chilled at that last image. But I remember, also, watching quietly the outline of the Americas, where generations of my ancestors had been born into lives of bondage and toil. Not a hint of colour there. Not even the weakest indication of belonging.

"Where are you from?" is a question I've been asked throughout my life, and most often by those who have been born and raised in Canada. I was asked it fairly recently, when we were together at the beach. As you know, I'm not a big fan of beaches or beach life. It's just not my thing, not really in my DNA, I'm tempted to explain, although it's true, people sometimes remind me, that both my parents are from the Caribbean. But it was one of those summer days in Vancouver when the damp and chill seem permanently banished, and the sky turns hot blue, and even I cannot help but be lured towards the sand and ocean. We had arranged to meet friends, but I ended up speaking with a friend of a friend, someone who quickly informed me that he worked in finance and now lived most of his time abroad. "But I was born and raised here," he asserted, before looking out onto the ocean and shaking his head. "Things are changing," he told me. "This *country* is changing. It's just not like it used to be even twenty years ago." He was not Indigenous, and so not someone who might hold a much deeper and more painful sense of change. He was not Asian, and so not someone historically targeted when white Vancouverites voice anxieties about change. I remember looking out at the ocean, focusing on the line where the distinct blues of sky and water met, until I heard the question, "Now, where did you say you're from again?" I explained, for the first time, that I had been living in this city for over a decade, but that I had been born and raised in Toronto. "No," said my beach companion, smiling. "Where are you *really* from?"

When I was little, I had a way of speaking that suggested to many that I was not *really* from Canada. The truth, however, was that I'd absorbed the Trinidadian accent of my parents, giving me a singing cadence and an inability, or else the unwillingness, to pronounce certain sounds. I remember how a primary school teacher noticed this, and how she booked me sessions with an in-school speech therapist. I remember one day leaving class under the watchful eyes of the other students and then waiting in an unusually cold office for the first session to begin. The speech therapist turned out to be kind, eager to help children like me say the right things the right way. On the first day, she pulled her chair close. She leaned her face in even closer to demonstrate a particular sound. "Thhhh ...," she hissed at me, her tongue slightly out and pressed between her teeth. "Thhhank you," she pronounced, "thhhhhhank you." Her breath wasn't good, and spit bubbled out between her teeth and worm-pink gums. It was the single most obscene thing I'd ever seen an adult do. I wouldn't have felt any more confused and disgusted if the therapist had tried to teach me how to fart.

I did, in the end, learn how to pronounce "th." Like others, I have made a concerted effort to speak in a way indistinguishable from other Canadians born here, although I do understand, of course, that many times it isn't my voice or what I say with it, but the louder silence of my body that suggests to others I am from elsewhere. I do sometimes wonder if you, of a very different generation and upbringing than me, have had similar experiences. If even now a girl like you can be asked, "Where are you *really* from?" or that worse question: "What *are* you?" Do you know, dearest daughter, that you also had a Trinidadian accent when you were younger? During your childhood, my parents helped raise you, and through this beautiful closeness you absorbed their way of speaking. You offered *tanks*. You gasped at the *tought* of seeing a *tousand* penguins. I

21

considered your way of speaking a gift, the proud evidence of an experience I never enjoyed, since, being the child of a certain class and generation of immigrants, I've never felt the warmth and closeness of grandparents. But when I remarked with pride to my father, "She speaks like you," he nodded gravely. "Don't worry," he reassured me. "She'll grow out of it."

For as long as I can remember, my parents yearned to be understood as simply Canadian, if not for themselves, then at least for their children and grandchildren. They knew, of course, who they were and where they came from. For good reasons, however, they were somewhat reluctant to declare their cultural or ancestral heritage either publicly or to strangers. They did once surprise me by doing just that. It happened before you were born and when your two sets of grandparents met for the first time. In many ways, your mother's parents could not be more different from mine. Your mother's father is an Oxford-trained professor of philosophy who worked at an elite Canadian university. Your mother's mother is a nationally renowned printmaker from a family of prominent business people and patrons of the arts. Both are multiple-generation white Canadians whom many middle-class people, never mind my parents, would consider intimidatingly sophisticated. My parents decided to offer a lunch, which they prepared with great care, not only because they had never before hosted people like your grandparents, but because hospitality is important to them, regardless of the guest. Out of their old glass cabinet came things reserved for special occasions. A heavy bowl of cut glass delicately dusted to hold the coleslaw. Something ambitiously called "silverware," but really just knives a little heavier and more polished than the ones we normally used, as well as forks with largely unbent tines. My mother carefully laid out White Swan napkins, purchased for the occasion, bright and soft with embossed designs at the edges.

Before the guests arrived, I did wonder how the conversation would go. Both of my parents grew up in Trinidad without a single book in their homes, and my mother in particular can get quite nervous around people she considers "cultured." She can find herself stumbling over words or descending nervously into quiet, forgetting all she has to offer. But your mother's parents, when they arrived, turned out to be exceptionally warm and "down to earth," as my parents afterwards pronounced. I know you love your mother's parents, and I also know that they love you, and I do sincerely believe that people of different backgrounds can learn to love one another. But I also believe that the acts of seeing and hearing are never automatic; and during that first lunch, when seated at the dining room table, there were, most definitely, more than a few moments of what your generation might term serious "awk." Your grandparents politely asked my parents about the Caribbean. What was Trinidad like in particular, they asked. Was this coleslaw Trinidadian cuisine? What were the native languages, the native customs? My mother tried, haltingly, to explain that she and her ancestors weren't really *native* to the Caribbean, that they had come ... been brought ... from elsewhere. The conversation shifted to your grandparents' parents, and the fact that your grandfather's mother had been a doctor, a remarkable achievement for a woman of the time. "And are there any doctors among your ancestors?" your grandmother asked politely. My mother looked quickly to her husband. My father finished chewing, neatly wiped his mouth with his White Swan napkin. "No," he answered. "No doctors. We were enslaved."

In 1498, upon his third voyage to what he imagined were the Indies, Christopher Columbus experienced uncertainty about the prospect of safely hitting land. After frightening days staring only at a watery horizon, he purportedly spotted three mountaintops, and in thanks to the Holy Trinity named the island Trinidad. My parents, at least, don't have any idea what three mountains Columbus might have seen. And so it is possible, as with all self-proclaimed discoverers of new lands and peoples, that Columbus saw only what he himself wished to see.

Trinidad was at that time densely populated by the Indigenous peoples the Arawak and the Caribs (from whom we get the name Caribbean). But through the brutalities of contact, the theft of resources, and European greed, many of them died and many were murdered. And soon after, another profound violence occurred. Over long centuries, African people were stolen from their homelands and transported across the Atlantic to work on plantations throughout the "New World," and especially in Trinidad and other parts of the Caribbean, to feed the growing European addiction for what we might now call "real cane sugar." An estimated ten to twelve million individuals were killed simply to make the business work. Many millions more survived for successive generations in conditions of living death. There is a story here of unimaginable cruelty and sorrow that we must nevertheless try to glimpse, not only because it is still an unrecognized human story but also because it is, in part, *our* story.

Recently, you proudly announced to us that you had read your first adult novel: Lawrence Hill's *The Book of Negroes*. It is a story about transatlantic slavery, though it is set in the U.S. and Canada, not the Caribbean. The book is told in the voice of a woman named Aminata, who as a child is stolen away from her family and community in Africa and with others shipped like cattle overseas. She bears witness to the murder of family members, friends, and acquaintances and to the lives of many more, including those of her very own children treated not as human beings but as property to be used and traded away. What helps her survive her terrible ordeals is a sense of herself as a *djeli*, a traditional teller and keeper of stories. Against the laws of the time, Aminata learns not only to read but also to write English, and thereby she comes to tell in her own voice a story of suffering but also of courage and resilience.

It is, in many ways, a discomforting novel for a girl of thirteen to read, and an essential one too. And what makes the experience extremely special is that you and your brother happen to know Aminata. Lawrence Hill gave his character the middle name of his oldest daughter. One day, when you were younger, he let me know that she was moving to Vancouver and would be in need of work to support her studies. Your mother and I were just then searching for childcare, since my parents had moved back to Toronto, and this is how you and your brother came to spend happy months with Geneviève Aminata Hill, one of the smartest and most radiant people we know. You could see, firsthand, why Lawrence was inspired to name his character after his eldest daughter.

There are other inspiring Black women in our life. Recently, we travelled to Toronto, just you and me, to attend a wedding between two of my dearest friends. You found yourself the only child in a restaurant filled with Black people and their friends, all laughing, eating, and carrying on. There were extravagant speeches. One of the toasters was a Black woman, a long-time organizer for the rights of Black people, queer people, and women and vulnerable workers in general. She raised her glass to the two newly married men, and she spoke of love and struggle and creativity as if they were natural and even necessary extensions of each other. At the end of her speech, she reminded us of a legacy. She called out the first names of writers, asking the crowd to remember and shout out the second. She called out Audre, and the crowd said, "Lorde." She called out Toni, and the crowd said, "Morrison." She called out Dionne, and this time you may have answered, "Brand." I know that, with the exception of the last, you might not have recognized all of the names, but I hope someday you will.

After her speech, the celebration continued. There was a DJ and there was wild dancing. The women present, the most brilliant people I'll ever know, kept asking you to dance with them. They were femme and butch, and they were cis and trans, and they were much, much more than I could see and attempt to describe, and they were all laughing at your athletic energy, and at the way you danced with quick feet and lifted arms, and also at the fact that, steaming hot though the place was, you wouldn't for a moment take off your black leather jacket. I think their desire to dance with you was a fierce insistence upon joy, and an expression of a still deeper commitment through thought and action against any power that would harm or control their bodies or yours.

You have always been "a tough girl," dearest daughter. You have never wanted help lifting something heavy; you have never admitted to anything being physically taxing, even when it was. You have never wanted me to conceal hard truths. I've actually confessed to you my fear, as a father, in admitting the following to you, and your response was, "But you *must*, because it matters." Remember how I felt chilled when we first viewed the heat map of my "maternal line"? Only the continent of Africa was lit up with concentrated colour, although my mother also has European heritage, as does her own mother and grandmother and still more distant ancestors. In that moment with you, I feared that the heat map of my "maternal line" indicated a long historical legacy of exclusively Black mothers with the occasional possibility of white fathers, but in the decades and centuries before sexual consent was possible for Black women. I feared that I was seeing in graphic form our ancestry as a story of recurring sexual violence. Such violence is an indisputable fact; but so too is the story of Black women surviving against incredible odds. And this is why we must together remain close to the women who dance, and promise always to keep learning from them.

★

"We were enslaved," my father once explained. But, in fact, this isn't true. His own ancestors were from South Asia, and they arrived in Trinidad as indentured workers in sugar cane and cocoa fields, which isn't the same thing as being enslaved, although indenture in the Caribbean was occasioned by the end of slavery, and it was yet another scheme by the powerful to build nations and amass wealth through the toil of others. Unlike slavery, the overseas migrations of the indentured were technically voluntary, although only the most desperate would undertake the journey; the voyages alone were sometimes deadly due to poor conditions on the ships.

Individuals would sign contracts binding them to their employers until their terms of work were fulfilled. But labourers could not always read the language of these contracts, and so there was the potential for bitter exploitation. Labourers could not leave their assigned plantations without a "ticket of leave," and those who broke even minor rules were subject to harsh penalties beyond the normal application of law. Few earned the money or independence they had hoped to obtain; many remained poor and estranged within lands they had never planned on settling. They were at least permitted to practise their culture—and this proved a source of strength. Over generations, ancient prayers would continue to be sung, and although the meanings of the words were sometimes forgotten, the effects of the sounds and music persisted. Groups that had once been enemies, or imagined between them divisions and hierarchies, now, through the hardships of a strange land, grew closer to each other, becoming *jahaji bhai*, or "ship brothers." Despite denigration, precious ways of understanding and proclaiming one's humanity would persist. My father remembers his own father walking over hot coals, transcending all pain through an enduring faith carried over wide and bitter seas.

But tensions inevitably arose between the newly arrived indentured workers and the recently freed slaves. Always remember, dearest daughter, that in the most meaningful sense, slavery was conquered not by laws and grand strokes of pens but through the heroism of Black people themselves, through the bravest acts of rebellion and demand, through everyday tactics of care and creativity. You can imagine how Black people might have felt when, having earned their freedom at enormous cost, and finally hoping for a fair share of the wealth and industries they had created, they watched as the owners of the plantations brought in workers from abroad. Understandably, each group—the formerly enslaved and the now or once indentured—believed they had already sacrificed too much and deserved much better. And it was all too easy for each group to imagine only the other as the cause of hardship and impoverishment, when in fact they needed to organize together against their oppressors.

A further impediment to working together was the enormous prejudice, throughout the Caribbean, based not only upon one's race but also upon the shade of one's skin. My mother tells stories about places where a brown paper bag was hung outside the door, and people were allowed entry only if their skin was judged lighter than the bag. As in many parts of the world where European racism has taken foot, one could simply look at a person and assume with almost perfect accuracy what he or she deserved, and where he or she fit in the hierarchies of society. And so even light-skinned Black people and light-skinned "Indians" could be contemptuous and dismissive of their own darker kin.

This history of race and colour is precisely why your grandparents are an unusual couple. My mother is a light-skinned Black person, which automatically gave her status; yet she was also the daughter of a single Black woman living in poverty, and thus scorned by the haughty Black middle class for being "illegitimate." My father is Indian, and of a broad category of people who would never have considered themselves Black; but he is of dark-skinned Tamil or "Madrassi" background, and thus thought to be on the very lowest rung of the hierarchies of caste and colour. Each of my parents had culturally ingrained reasons to be suspicious of the other "racial" group. But each also had personal reasons not to feel fully accepted by their own communities.

In eventually growing close to each other, my parents left behind them the habits of their own families and communities; they would continue their journey together, travelling to Canada, where, ironically, in the early days of immigration, their "racial" difference would rarely be observed or acknowledged. For good or bad, they became just two more "coloured" people. My father knows very well that he is not of African ancestry, but I've watched him get uncontrollably angry when witnessing discrimination against Black people, and in these moments I've heard him announce himself as "Black too," and with his raised voice and shaved head I have seen him assumed to be so. My mother, in turn, gave up her maiden name, Boiselle, which to some carried with it a nice ring of European "class," proudly adopting instead what some of her more pretentious family members worried was an unseemly "coolie" name.

"What *kind* of name is that?" is another question I often get, and maybe you do too. I'm told the name is of South Indian and Tamil origin, although ultimately I don't know. Generations ago, either when arriving in the Caribbean or else departing for it, one of your ancestors no doubt spoke the name to a colonial scribe, who in turn wrote down an approximation of what he heard. As such, it is a name very likely corrupted, although it is also a name that marks both memory and survival against the odds. Many decades ago, your great-grand-father on my father's side wished to send his children to a good school in Trinidad, but he was informed that, in order to receive such an education, his children would have to change their last name to a proper Christian one. Your great-grandfather faced a painful dilemma. The school offered his children the glimmer of hope for a life beyond the tough one that he and his own ancestors had endured. In the end, my grandfather agreed to the requirement and, slyly or not, chose for his children the last name Thomas, after the one disciple in the Bible who openly doubts. But when his children grew close to adulthood, he changed his mind. He officially switched back the names of his male children, spending a considerable portion of his life's savings to do so. That name, Chariandy, is the one you now carry, and like the specific beauty of your body, you should be proud of it, for both were passed on to you by our ancestors at a very unfair price.

What is the real story, the truest *meaning*, of our origins? What significance does the birthplace of my parents hold for people like you and me? Not long ago, we went to Trinidad as a family, all six of us. For my parents, having reached their eighties, it was imagined as a last trip to the place they once called home. For you, your brother, and also your mother, it was a first visit to a fabled land.

When raising you, my parents told you stories about the Trinidad of their childhood: the murky ravine they swam in; the saltfish and "ground provisions" miraculously stretched to feed large families during the war; the simple, hand-built homes with corrugated iron roofs that funnelled rainwater for washing; the dirt streets filled with people and with life. "It's all gone now," my mother whispered to me on the flight there. "Almost all of my family has passed away. Even the homes and streets have been bulldozed. What will we show them?"

But, in fact, they showed us much. They named for us hibiscus, and chenette, and more varieties of mango than we could remember. They identified the cute and clumsy-looking creature, a cross between a rodent and a very small pig, that managed to sprint up an impossibly steep hill. It was an agouti. And when my father joked about how agoutis taste in a stew, you immediately threatened to stew *him*. "Everyone looks like us," you said to me once, squeezing my arm and smiling as we walked in a park. I think we both knew this wasn't quite true, and that the people around us were each beautiful in very different ways. But it was true enough that, for the first time together, we had stepped into a country where, upon a glance, we might be assumed to *really* belong.

But we did not belong, dearest daughter, not actually. We had come back not as the struggling people my parents had been, nor as contemporary Trinidadians whether poor or not, but as Canadians on vacation, and with only the worries sprung by our nation's official travel advisory regarding the crime that inevitably flourishes whenever generations of people have been exploited and denied opportunity. We had "returned" as tourists, and yet not just as tourists but as people with connections through music, food, and language, people bearing precious stories of life and struggles "there."

Years ago, I tried to put this complicated heritage into words, and I wrote a book looking back to a Caribbean past from the perspective of someone raised in Canada, someone whose "memories" of his ancestral homeland were provided by a mother now in a state of forgetting. "My history is a foreign word," the narrator of my novel says in a mood of exasperation. But readers and writers who lived in the Caribbean appeared interested in my book. They felt, as I did, a certain connection. And this is how, years before our "return" as a family, I was invited to Trinidad as a judge for a literary prize and to participate in a festival celebrating Caribbean literature. During that trip, I met writers with ties to other parts of the Caribbean, and one magical night we each read from our work at an elegant little bookstore. In different ways, we voiced the histories and futures of this brutal, beautiful "ground zero" of the Americas. We read very late into the night, and after it was over we were hungry. Someone suggested a roadside roti stand still open in a sketchy part of Saint James, where we had been warned not to go at night. But we were desperate, and in numbers, and so we climbed into a couple of cabs.

I had expected a small shop of some sort, but the roti stand turned out to be nothing more than a small gas stove and a stack of coolers and bags at the side of a busy but poorly lit road. Working there was a lone woman with her two young children. I watched as she received our orders without any indication that she had heard them. "Slight pepper, please," I asked her, in the way I had learned in Canada, and she continued cooking with her sure bare fingers on the smoking griddle, her eyes squinting, her long straight hair loosely bundled upon her head. I watched her two kids, even younger than I had first thought, toddling around unsupervised a few yards away at the side of the dark road. There was no real sidewalk where they could play, and the cars raced by on the crumbling asphalt at what seemed to me a reckless speed. You were young at the time, your brother was even younger, and I suddenly imagined how frightened I would be knowing that the two of you and your mother were out alone like this late at night, in a sketchy neighbourhood and vulnerable in many ways to hurt, not from any lack of love, but because this was how a loving mother was able to provide for her children.

Eventually, the rotis were ready, and they were delicious. It was for me another encounter with art, with craft and knowledge carried overseas from a long-forgotten continent and filled with the oftentimes scarce ingredients of the New World. It was an intimate experience of food and of memory. And it was also an experience of detachment, of the feeble pity you sometimes feel when observing people you think are distant from you. But then a new friend and fellow writer joked, "You gobbled that roti *fast*, *fast*, Mr. Chariandy," and the woman looked up from her stove for the first time. "My mother was a Chariandy. We are related," she said, and turned back to her stove. And when I looked at her children, they were each watching me very carefully.

You did not create the inequalities and injustices of this world, daughter. You are neither solely nor uniquely responsible to fix them. If there is anything to learn from the story of our ancestry, it is that you should respect and protect yourself; that you should demand not only justice but joy; that you should see, *truly* see, the vulnerability and the creativity and the enduring beauty of others. Today, many years after indenture and especially slavery, there are many who continue to live painfully in wakes of historical violence. And there are current terrible circumstances whereby others, in the desperate hope for a better life, either migrate or are pushed across the hardened borders of nations and find themselves stranded in unwelcoming lands. We live in a time, dearest daughter, when the callous and ignorant in wealthy nations have made it their business to loudly proclaim who are the deserving "us" (those *really* "us") and who are the alien and undeserving "them." But the story of our origins offers us a different insight. The people we imagine most apart from "us" are, oftentimes, our own forgotten kin.

THE INCIDENT

Spring came and with it change. In your last weeks of elementary school, you insisted on walking home alone, letting yourself in with your own key, and baking cookies and muffins from recipes drawn solely from your head, heavy on the chocolate chips. One afternoon, you visited a thrift shop with your girlfriends and brought back steel-grey jeans and a pink hoodie. "*Pink*," I remarked, the first time I saw you wear it, and you shrugged while stirring batter in a bowl. The rains let up, the air got warmer, the sky lighter. Each lengthening evening, we watched from our balcony the crows leafing through the air towards their unknown roosting site. "A murder," said your mother. "That's what they're called in a flock. Listen, can you hear?" You listened before nodding. Your brother nodded too. I was last to catch them, the whisper-quiet of wings above the noise of a city. The summer break drew near, and, in that last week of school, your brother was called a nigger.

I didn't think he'd ever be called that. He'd always possessed what I'd imagined to be ambiguous features. People often tell me "he looks like you," but this only complicates matters. My own brother of the same mother and father looks unambiguously Black. And as a child, I was considered Black too. But through the unpredictability of genetic inheritance, and perhaps the thinning and loosening of my curls with age, these days I am often asked about my background. Ethiopian, Sudanese, and South Indian people wonder if I'm the same as them. Some born in Trinidad, or having knowledge of the place, smilingly call me a Dougla, a word for a person of mixed African and South Asian descent.

Of course, the circumstance is even less clear for both you and your brother, children of a white mother, children undeniably "of colour," to use the ridiculous language of the now and here, with brown skin, curly hair, and dark eyes—but what more specifically? I have tried to instill in both of you a strong sense of pride regarding your African and South Asian ancestry, knowing that one may very easily be made to feel otherwise. But the fact is that I've never actually named you one way or the other, never told you, authoritatively, what you are, racially speaking. I suppose that I have imagined, at times, that you, as such complexly mixed children, might have the opportunity to choose and declare your own identity. I had forgotten that racial identity is so rarely a matter of personal choice. That it is always, in origin, a falsehood and violence, though it can become, all the same, a necessary tool for acknowledging the enduring life and creativity of a persistently maligned people.

At the time of what soon came to be called "the incident," your brother had been having a hard year at school. He was struggling academically and having serious difficulties concentrating on his work. He felt frustrated and down, and one teacher, the year before, suggested that "toughening up" was required of a boy like him. This strategy resulted in nothing more than mysterious stomach aches and ailments and deepening anxieties about school. During recess and lunch, your brother would roam the playground alone, dreading the return to his desk.

And then the incident. A girl accompanied by her friends sought out your brother and called him the word. "Don't call me that," your brother managed to say, understanding the insult. "You can't tell me what to call you," the girl answered. For the rest of day, your brother felt more down than ever. But it was all witnessed and reported, and the clunky machinery of a school committed to the vague ideal of diversity—or at least afraid of being embarrassed—went into effect. A message was left on our home phone, acknowledging that "an incident" had happened, reassuring us that it was being addressed. The girl was questioned by the principal, and her parents were contacted. In the midst of my own bitter feelings, I'll confess that my thoughts did go to that relatively young girl, and to the confusion she might be experiencing, having doubtlessly known she was being mean, but perhaps now confused by everyone's reaction. After all, she had done little more than absorb and relay a message freely circulating in the world.

The following day, you handled the situation. That you were prepared to confront the girl and her friends wasn't all that surprising to me. What was surprising is that, in confronting the girl and her friends, you were accompanied by a boy. For years, you had had very little time for boys, finding them not particularly bright or interesting, certainly not as athletic as you, never able to better you in push-ups or foot races. During your last week in elementary school, you would not have needed a boy for "muscle." And so I don't know through what quietly existing relationship and agreement the two of you together approached the offending girl and her friends. I can see the two of you standing there. The boy, white, concerned, but quiet because he might have known intuitively that this wasn't his time to speak, or perhaps you told him outright not to do so. You, a brown-skinned girl with eyes like fired coals. "Don't you *ever* call my brother that again," you told the girl. She managed a tight nod.

That was how you handled the incident. But how did we as parents? Your mother was very angry. It was the anger of someone who had never been named the way your brother was, but who has known, as a woman, other damaging labels. I'm happy both that she revealed her anger and that you saw it. Never let anyone tell you that as a girl, you shouldn't express how angry you are. I was angry too, but, later that evening, when we gathered as a family, I wanted to speak from something other than that emotion. For some vague and unspoken reason, we had decided, all four of us, to sit on the polished wooden floor of the living room, everyone except the notoriously inflexible me sitting fairly comfortably. In this already awkward position, I wanted to explain something to your brother, but also to you and your mother, something of vital importance, something I'd been meaning to tell you for a long time about the experience of being named. But now, as the opportunity presented itself, I was failing. I tried again and again. I kept swallowing and clearing my throat, noticing both you and your brother glancing at me but trying not to stare.

As you know, I've developed the habit of turning to literature to help make sense out of life. And there is, coincidentally enough, a poem by Countee Cullen entitled "Incident." It was published over ninety years ago, and it is about a boy who is happily sightseeing in the city of Baltimore until he is abruptly called nigger. It's a deceptively simple poem, in which the surprise and pain of the naming is artfully evoked within the directness of language and the tick-tock reliability of the rhymes. It's not such a stretch to assume, at least for a moment, that the poem is based upon a real experience. And if it is, then the poem is a minor victory, for Cullen has in the end managed to convey to others, in the form of his choosing, both an experience and its psychological effect. But the poem also suggests that the cost of being named is, potentially, to forget everything else. In a way, the cost of being named is life itself.

Incident

Once riding in old Baltimore,
Heart-filled, head-filled with glee,
I saw a Baltimorean
Keep looking straight at me.

Now I was eight and very small,
And he was no whit bigger,
And so I smiled, but he poked out
His tongue, and called me, "Nigger."

I saw the whole of Baltimore
From May until December,
Of all the things that happened there
That's all that I remember.

—Countee Cullen

I was raised not in Countee Cullen's United States, in a time and place that some imagine perfectly remote from ours. I was born in a nation that for more than two hundred years has imagined itself substantially different from its southern neighbour and yet must reckon with its own painful histories. In 1963, my parents' race and country of origin were enough to bar them from entering Canada, but nevertheless they managed to come here, performing hard work that few here were willing to do in order to provide opportunities for themselves and their children. At first, they lived in downtown Toronto near other people from the Caribbean. But after I was born, they scraped together a down payment for a modest townhouse in the far southeast of what was then the city of Scarborough. The neighbourhood where my brother and I grew up was considered, self-consciously, a "good" part of Scarborough, mostly featuring bungalows and detached two-storey homes with manicured lawns. It was populated overwhelmingly by middle-class white people. The child of working-class Black and Brown parents, I was very noticeable, not only for how I looked but for how I spoke and acted, what I wore and possessed. As I grew up, your country as a whole, but also Scarborough in particular, was increasingly being settled by racial-minority immigrants, who by then were more freely allowed to enter. But out of old and enduring forms of ignorance, not everyone was comfortable with these changes, these new presences in the neighbourhood, and so I grew up the embodiment of what some feared and refused to understand.

Many times, in my "good" neighbourhood, I was called a nigger. I could have been called other names. If I had grown up in Trinidad, I might have been called a Dougla. If I had grown up elsewhere, in London, England, for instance, or in another global city boasting deeper and richer histories of South Asian immigration, I might have been called a Paki; and, in fact, I remember a couple times roaming beyond my neighbourhood, my hair cut short, when I was. But in the Scarborough of my time, I was most often called a nigger, or a jungle bunny or a spear chucker. Passing groups of boys on a sidewalk, walking warily through a strip mall or down a suddenly narrowing school hallway, I knew I could be pushed or tripped, that stuff could be thrown at me. Twice, vividly, I felt the thin, wet splat of spit on my scalp, and when I turned I saw a group of boys chuckling, though I was unable to tell which boy had been bold and bad enough to perform the act. A good chunk of my energy and attention as a child was devoted to monitoring the physical presence of people around me, reading smiles for potentially wicked intentions, bracing when I heard about me laughter.

I'm sure there were moments when I misjudged people, when laughter was just laughter, when a smile wasn't a threat. I'm sure that some of the people who freely spoke that word were not always consciously malicious. I played with those who chanted "Eeny, meeny, miny, moe, catch a nigger by the toe" to assign roles in a game of hide-and-seek, never realizing that long ago, in a deeper way, I had already been determined "it." I cheered for football teams alongside schoolmates who might shout down players on the opposing team by calling them niggers, or else brag to others about travelling outside of the neighbourhood to "egg niggers," only then noticing, with an embarrassed smile, who was standing among them. I was invited to play along with my friends when they would imitate the jive talk and silly gestures of Black comedians they saw on television and in movies, not appreciating that these comedians were trying, at least at times, to reveal more complex and serious truths about the roles they were expected to perform both on stage and in life. And my friends would be disappointed, even puzzled, if I didn't enthusiastically join in.

But the truth, dearest daughter, is that I sometimes did play along. I didn't want them to know when I was hurt. I was afraid that if others recognized my vulnerability, the racist insults and bullying would only intensify. Perhaps even at that young age I had already learned to be "a man," to not admit to myself or others any stupid sensitivities. Perhaps I sought, like some of the comedians I watched, to play along in the dim hope of ultimately tricking up the role.

A practical consequence of all this was the deterioration of my relationship with school. I remember vividly the summer days leading up to my first year of high school. I was particularly excited about learning French, about entering the world of a whole new language. I got my hands on a library book of verb conjugations and began memorizing them in preparation for the first class of the year. But when I showed up, the teacher immediately read me as trouble and forced me to sit at the front of the class where she could, she warned, keep an eye on me. For days afterwards, known to her or not, I was pelted with bits of pink eraser, with spitballs blown through empty pen tubes, which would either bounce off my hair or get lost in what others saw as the jungled tangles. The word "nigger" was whispered. Soon, I demonstrated quite perfectly what my French teacher had suspected all along—my inability to focus effectively in the classroom, my willingness to disrupt the lessons with frustrated outbursts and jokiness, my failure, eventually, to regularly attend class.

Once, however, in another class, a supply teacher did notice the relatively open behaviour of certain boys towards me. Shocked, she sent these boys to the principal's office. Some of the students who remained in the class were equally shocked. They couldn't understand why the supply teacher, a white woman, was being so "bitchy." "Do *you* think they deserved to be punished?" they wanted to know. "Do *you* think it's fair?" Fair or not, when the boys returned to class, they had an important message for me. "We asked the principal," one told me, "if it would be all right if you called us honkies. If you'd be punished if *you* were the one who called *us* names." I'd never called any of them honkies. Not because I was morally superior, but simply because I understood, very clearly, that coming from a Black boy in an overwhelmingly white class and school, this word wouldn't stick or damage in any real way. However, for both the boys and the principal, this nuance regarding power and language was very much beside the point. It was more important and psychologically convenient to reassure everyone that *no* form of racism would be tolerated. "You'd be in serious, *serious* trouble," the boy rightly warned me, jutting his finger at me.

There is an effect in being named, whether one is a "nigger" or a "Paki," whether one is a "Chink" or a "bitch," a "faggot" or "fat" or "trash" or any other number of words that are not equivalent, not exchangeable, but nevertheless, even on the quiet of this page, and in my effort now to be honest and protective, inevitably hurt and implicate. There is a toll upon the self. It was easy for me to believe that I was indeed trouble, or a joker, that I was untrustworthy in basic ways, a predator and a pervert despite my shyness, that I really wasn't cut out for school, or for serious thought in general. I had little concept of a future, and imagined that at some fundamental level, there was something unpleasant about me, an oily smell not entirely attributable to the strange foods my parents served, but a secretion from my body, from my skin itself.

At the same time, I understood very well that the hurtful people around me were never monsters of the Hollywood-movie type. The boy who regaled us with nigger jokes might also choose me first for his team. The girl who scorned me, laughed about me with her friends, might also tell me during a chance encounter in an empty school stairwell that, actually, it wasn't true that I was ugly. I glimpsed their contradictions, their inner doubts and vulnerabilities, their brave curiosities and cowardly tribalisms, their sincere desire to be good and also their ability to be casually cruel. The truth is that before I could appreciate my own complex humanity, I was made to understand and appreciate *theirs*, which I saw confirmed, over and over again, on television, in films, and in books.

I did want a life of my own in books. I wanted to read, and, mysteriously, even scandalously, I wanted to write. Your grandmother will attest that at a very early age, perhaps nine or ten, I secretly informed her I wanted to live alone in a log cabin in the woods and write. I can hear you laughing as you read this, knowing as you do that I never seek out experiences in "nature," and hold no romantic notions about living even temporarily away from electricity and hot running water. But I think, as a child, I had a fantasy about retreating from the heated language around me, from the words launched at me in hallways and streets, hissed at me from radios, televisions, and newspapers in their coverage of people who looked like me. I wanted different terms for living in language, and like any other child, I had discovered a particular, even peculiar, passion.

Few around me considered my passion appropriate. Early on in high school, a teacher explained to my parents that I demonstrated no academic ability. He suggested that I withdraw from advanced courses and instead pursue a trade. My parents, of course, saw no disappointment in the idea of a trade. A trade would have been a significant step up from minding children and working in a non-unionized factory. And a trade, of course, can be a beautiful means of pursuing a passion— just not mine. I was about to be routed to general studies or a trade school, but at the last moment, a guidance counsellor dug up my standardized tests. Every indicator of intellectual aptitude, she discovered, was significantly above average, and my reading comprehension, affirmed time and time again at different grade levels, was at the absolute highest on the scale. "Do you know you're smart?" the counsellor asked, looking at me over the rim of her glasses. I remember not answering for a long time. I remember trying to read her blue eyes, as if this might be just another cruel joke.

Of course, I wasn't unique in the neighbourhood. There were other kids negotiating their special visibility as East Asian children, South Asian children, Arab children, Indigenous children. Two sisters lived a few doors down from me in the townhouse complex. They had a Black father but were raised by their white mother, who was a teacher. The sisters did very well in school. Both were beautiful, and I was drawn in particular to the one who would sail by me on blue roller skates.

But we always kept our distance. Certainly, there was that long stretch of time when neighbourhood boys and girls, in general, stopped playing together. And I was also, for various reasons, painfully shy about approaching girls. For much of my childhood, I would walk past that girl, matching what I felt was a certain remoteness in her eyes, watching but not *looking* like I was watching. I found myself wondering what she might be thinking and feeling. I did not suspect that she would one day become a writer and give me and others a powerful sense of what her own upbringing was like.

To be a person of colour is to be marked in a peculiar kind of way. You are at once highly visible—obvious, conspicuous, apparent. Yet at the same time you are virtually invisible—unseen, overlooked, transparent. Children, I think, share this strange experience— they are to be seen and not heard, they are spoken *of*, and spoken *for*, but not often spoken to. As a child of colour, I experienced this silencing effect while also enduring racial slights and slurs from strangers and family members alike. By the time I reached my teen years, I knew how to disappear in order to avoid unwanted attention, and I knew how to de-race myself in order to make "the majority" feel more at ease. I might have learned these lessons from the steady flow of books in which I immersed myself; certainly, young Black women were almost never featured in these narratives, and those who did appear were relegated to the margins or permitted to fill only the most demeaning roles.

—Zetta Elliott

Of course, the child closest to me was my younger brother, though many assume he is my *big* brother. Your uncle is today one of the most thoughtful, sensitive, and generous people you and I know. In his life and work, he prides himself on his ability to listen, to be diplomatic, to de-escalate situations, and in these ways to gain the trust of those seeking help. But at a young age, it seemed to him that advertising these empathic qualities would be extremely unwise for a boy like him. If the world was going to be tough to a Black working-class kid, then that kid was going to be tough right back. In his early teens, he began to muscle up, working out with men at hardcore gyms, drinking blender jugs full of raw eggs (can you believe he's a vegan now?), and developing around himself—both body and soul—an impenetrable carapace. Recently, I was looking at old photos of my brother, and I noticed the changing face he presented to the world, from a joyful child, to a boy with an increasingly self-conscious smile, to a youth still beautiful, still secretly thoughtful and empathetic, but aiming out to any watcher his scowling game face on a bulked-up, ripped, hardened body.

My best friend throughout my childhood was a Black boy who lived in the same townhouse complex and whose parents were also hard-working people from the Caribbean. In the security of our friendship, he could joke about his family in a Bajan accent just as I could joke about mine in a Trini one. While the kids around us wore concert shirts featuring AC/DC and Ozzy Osbourne and Rush, we somehow discovered the long-dead Jimi Hendrix, and assured ourselves that *he* was the greatest hard rock guitarist ever. We got our hands on golf clubs, and in school fields we played tournaments, imagining ourselves Calvin Peete, the only Black golfer we knew. Once, my friend came back from a summer in Barbados with tales of a game called road tennis, and we got to work playing it ourselves, cutting wooden paddles from a sheet of plywood, creating a net from a long, foot-high board, and chalking out a smallish court on the asphalt playground in our townhouse complex. We reluctantly admitted we were geeks, and with other social outcasts of different backgrounds we escaped into long Dungeons & Dragons campaigns, dreaming up adventure and heroism for ourselves in lands long ago and far away. My friend and I read fantasy voraciously, the good and the bad, ignoring as best we could how almost always the dark-skinned monsters were vanquished by the fair. In the late eighties, when we were older and could freely travel out of our neighbourhood, we connected with youths from more diverse parts of Scarborough, and together we found in hip hop the styles and rhythms and language and postures that seemed, in the moment, to promise us lives both bigger and bolder than what others had imagined for us.

We did not come from the "hoods" evoked in the music we enjoyed. We were not "gangstas" from asphalt jungles, but were children whose parents had sacrificed a lot to place us here, in a "good" neighbourhood, in reach of "good" schools, and in a land they believed to be one of genuine opportunity. And still, as Black youths we faced what even our parents couldn't always see: the clutched purses of women when we approached; the watchful assumptions of cashiers when we entered a store; the constant, everyday assumptions of adults about our intelligence, our moral character, our bodies. Sometimes we resisted, understanding in doing so the special risk we faced from authorities. Other times we could do little more than meet eyes, exchange a knowing glance, a covert smile, a private joke—small, careful gestures that said, "Hey, I see you. I get it."

But they take a toll, these indications in both life and culture, that you don't belong here, not really, that you are distasteful and immediately suspect, that speech and thought are not expected of you. Once, after a particularly miserable English class, my friend joked that he would someday write a poem about his hand. "This right here," he said, and he held up his fingers in a posture of outlandish reverence, so *gay* we might have joked stupidly then. Imagining a poem like this, about the beauty of a Black boy's hand, we laughed loudly, uncontrollably, until, suddenly, we stopped.

When, eventually, I was admitted to university, I found myself alone. My parents, of course, had not gone to university. But it seemed more than a coincidence that none of the Black boys I was closest to went either: not my best friend, whom I had always considered smarter and more creative than me; not the neighbour a few doors down, the adopted brother of the sisters I mentioned; not the cool brothers a couple years apart in high school, one a master at breakdancing, the other obsessed with country music; not even the boy from the facing row of townhouses who was a year ahead of me in school and had once acted a bit like an older brother, a smart and athletic kid now rumoured, rightly or not, to be heavily into drugs.

My university in the nation's capital then had a modest reputation, and against all apparent reason, I declared my major to be English. In my first class, I sat apart, observing myself to be the lone Black person in the room, not an unfamiliar experience, and one I would confront over and over again. During that first semester, as the snowy Ottawa winter settled in, I went on long night walks, bundled up against the cold, and finding further anonymity in my gloves and hooded parka, in the scarf that all but covered my face. I haunted the university library, walking among stacks of books, rows upon rows of them, awed by all that writing, and feeling a strange sense of possibility.

I know a lot of privileged people who claim there is no "practical" value in a humanities degree. These people seem to see little that is worthwhile in thinking and reading widely about what it means to be human. Conversely, I have rarely heard these disparaging claims from working people like my parents, who themselves never went to university—people whose humanity is not automatically taken for granted, and who know what it feels like to be consigned, upon sight, to a life of strict "practicalities." I do know, intimately now, that universities are but an aspect of society as a whole, and echo, most disappointingly, its many problems. But I also know that it was only through my university classes that I was exposed to new worlds. I discovered the open magic of literature, the rewards of reading beyond borders and cultures, beyond identity and race, beyond any idea of who you are and what you are meant to be.

Yet I also craved writing that would speak more specifically to me. One night, I pulled almost randomly from a library shelf *The Price of the Ticket*, the collected essays of James Baldwin. I thumbed my way to an essay entitled "Stranger in the Village," about Baldwin's stay in a remote Swiss village and how, only there, in a condition of estrangement, was he able to reflect upon his experiences as a Black man in both America and Europe, and upon the world as a whole. Baldwin's writing touched me like nothing else had before. I didn't even find myself a chair; I sat right there on the worn carpet in the stacks, mesmerized by what and how he wrote.[1]

---

1 "No road whatever will lead Americans back to the simplicity of this European village where white men still have the luxury of looking on me as a stranger. I am not, really, a stranger any longer for any American alive.... This world is white no longer, and it will never be white again." —James Baldwin, "Stranger in the Village."

Gradually, over my years at university, I fell into the company of people I wouldn't otherwise have met: international students from Africa, Europe, South Asia, and the Caribbean; women of all backgrounds unashamed of calling themselves feminists; queer people of different genders. I began learning (and I am still today learning) of the gazes that fall upon the bodies of other vulnerable people, and of the need to share these experiences. But the strongest connections I made then were with Black men who had likewise come from suburbs, "good" or "bad," and who were often the children of immigrant parents who had not themselves gone to university. We scraped together our tuition and rent and made do with meals of pasta and jars of Ragú sauce, spicy condiments brought from home, and grade C chicken that had passed its expiration date. We all had different passions and programs of study, different likes and dislikes, but each of us, every one, had stories to tell of friends who were brighter, maybe even brighter than us, but who hadn't "made it." They were kids from loving if struggling homes like ours, but with a sick parent whose illness had plunged the household into chaos. They were kids busted and sentenced for minor drug offences; kids who had grown both bitter and sensitive and who had come to permanently hurt themselves or others in fruitless fights over "reputation"; kids jailed, or expelled from school, or else, through the everyday erosion of hope in society and belief in themselves, had simply come to question whether they had a livable future.

One of my roommates was a big guy, with the sort of shy-gentle eyes I felt I'd known all my life. One cold winter night, when we were fixing ourselves a supper of fried eggs, he shared with me and our two other housemates a story. He had been driving in his old neighbourhood when he was pulled over by the cops for a routine check. This had happened before, but this time, when the cops walked up to the window of the car, they seemed to misjudge my friend reaching to unbuckle his seatbelt to fish out his ID. "*Gun!*" shouted one of the cops, and both of them drew weapons and aimed at close range. "I thought I was dead," he told us. "I *heard* the gunshot, I *smelled* the gunpowder. It was real, you know? It actually *happened*, just not that time to me." We were quiet for a while after that. We all understood. The possibilities that were not mere possibilities. The fates that were not our fates but might easily have been so.

We woke to the stench of cheap margarine burning in a pan, and one roommate jumped up to turn off the stove, another to open the window. Our dinner was ruined, our precious kitchen heat quickly disappearing, but my roommate with the shy-gentle eyes was laughing all the same. What was so funny? "We made it here," he explained. We stared at him before realizing it was true. We had found allies. We'd found each other. We were

61

lucky, though none of this had happened by accident. It had demanded empathetic neighbours and teachers. It had demanded the work and undaunted love of parents. It had required the persistence of a message, an old message stretching back generations to some anonymous distant ancestor who dared whisper into a child's ear, "You are not what they see and say you are. You are more." My roommate stood there with a silly smile on his face. Soon we were all wearing it.

Before the birth of both you and your brother, dearest daughter, these were the most beautiful smiles I'd ever seen.

Years later, while waiting for a train in the city of my birth, I felt a slap on my back and I started in the way I've never really learned to overcome. "*Cherry-monkey!*" a man exclaimed—an old nickname of mine, and certainly not the worst. He recognized me as a classmate from the old days, and he began to reminisce. He talked about fine old days in the neighbourhood when "everyone got along," and when people's lives weren't so complicated by "politics." He talked about the prom, not quite aware that I hadn't attended. He reminded me of what a joker I had been, what a little schemer. "*Cherry-f***ing-monkey,*" he said, beaming, slapping me again on the shoulder. "Right here again in front of me—*completely* unbelievable!" And it's true, dearest daughter.

It's more than a bit unbelievable the way I've ended up, the life I'm able to provide for you, since you must know it could easily have been otherwise. In modest ways, through my efforts both as a teacher and especially as a writer, I have managed, at least at times, to answer back in terms of my choosing to the voices that once paralyzed me with doubt.

And so has your brother. Shortly after "the incident," your brother was diagnosed with significant writing output challenges and he began working with a teacher of the sort you've always liked. She had a no-nonsense, almost brutally honest style—something I associated, rightly or not, with the teacher's "old-school" Caribbean background. But I'll confess I was at first worried that this sort of teacher might not be right for your brother. I was concerned about him feeling discouraged or, worse, humiliated. But your brother responded well to this particular type and source of toughness and to the teacher's refusal to accept from him anything less than his best effort. About a week after starting with her, he returned home with a handwritten prose poem, "A beautiful winter morning." "I did it all by myself," he told me proudly. He had managed to do what he hadn't before thought interesting or even possible. And, here especially, I'm tempted to believe that he accomplished even more. Being named, he found his own voice. Being sighted, he learned, nevertheless, to see.

A beautiful winter morning

The air was fresh, and cold. It was sunny and the sky was intense blue. The snow was dazzling and brilliant white. Across the field, towering trees cast shadows over the bushes. The only footprints were those of the birds, who were singing a melody, as if celebrating winter. I touched my fingertips to the snow. It was crisp, but soft. I sighed, and found that for the first time in a long time, I had found a beautiful day.

THE ARRIVAL

Once when you were five, I was invited to Berlin. This was an honour for me as a relatively inexperienced writer. I was hesitant to leave your mother by herself with two very young children, although I also confess, dearest daughter, that as a new parent I did look forward to a few days alone. I've never been an easy traveller, but I need to tell you that on that particular trip I experienced nothing at all unpleasant. I was not pulled aside for special questioning and screening, perhaps because I wasn't wearing the clothes and didn't possess a

65

last name that signalled a faith deemed threatening. Arriving in Germany, I produced for the border official a passport declaring my citizenship to a country categorized as developed and safe. I spoke English, and in it introduced myself not only as an invited guest but also a professor whose novel had been translated into German. When I was waved through by the uninterested border official, I felt something that I do not always possess, but certainly sometimes do, especially today. It is something called privilege.

I had been invited to Germany to visit the Literary Colloquium Berlin, and when I arrived, I was a bit shocked by the grandness of the old mansion, its wood fixtures and mouldings, its slightly sour smell, perhaps of lacquer or of old wood. I happened to visit at a time when no other writers were staying in the guest quarters, and I was assigned an alarmingly fine suite with an office overlooking a lake. I spent every spare moment of my three-day stay in that office, working intensely on a draft of a novel, trying to make the best use of this precious time. When I needed to rest my eyes, I looked out on the lake, which was grey and olive beneath the overcast sky and like a painting in its stillness. When I needed a walk, I visited a nearby forest, its paths carpeted with leaves, its trees bare and black and wet. It rained throughout my visit, but it was one of those soft rains I had grown accustomed to from winters spent in

Vancouver. During my walks through the German forest, or along the roads by the lake, the rain offered me welcome solitude and anonymity. It seemed to discourage others from strolling about, and my umbrella acted as a sort of canopy, absorbing sound, limiting my view of the surroundings and encouraging me to focus inward on the challenges of voice and form in my new book.

The only time I experienced significant company was during an evening when I was interviewed about my first novel, which, as you know, tells the story of a woman afflicted with dementia. I spoke about the specific sorrows of that condition, but also about the bigger question of cultural memory, about the often-forgotten pasts of migrant peoples and historically persecuted minorities. I remember this explanation not because it was in any way original or compelling, but because of what I discovered on the day of the interview.

Shortly before taking the stage, I had dinner with the staff of the Colloquium and some other people from Berlin's writing and publishing scene, including a representative from my publisher, Suhrkamp Verlag, a press that was, among its many distinctions, launched in Frankfurt in 1949 by a Jewish survivor of a concentration camp. The representative from Suhrkamp was from the American South, and we talked about many things. At one point, he asked how it felt to be staying at the Colloquium. I said that I had found the accommodation almost embarrassingly luxurious and that everyone had treated me very nicely, but I sensed instantly that my response was inadequate, that I was somehow missing the point. It was only after the talk that I found out what it was, first from two friends who happened to be living in Berlin and then, later that night, sitting alone in my suite, searching the internet. I remember looking up from my computer and into the window, and this time seeing only my face lit up and reflected in the darkened glass, and not the lake outside, which I had only just learned was named Wannsee.

On January 20, 1942, in a nearby villa sharing the view of the lake whose serenity and beauty I had enjoyed while writing, the Wannsee Conference took place, attended by various senior officials of the Nazi regime who gathered to address what they officially called "The Final Solution to the Jewish Question." We know of this from carefully censored minutes of the conference, and from the direct testimony of Adolf Eichmann himself. During his interrogation in 1962, Eichmann admitted that the minutes were missing the very blunt discussions that had taken place about the participants' ambitions for the "liquidation" and "extermination" of the Jews of Europe. The Holocaust had begun, in fact, before the Wannsee Conference, but the conference was a turning point, when active practice and ingrained ideology became invested with newfound political authority and official language.

I was grateful to have learned all this. I believe that however much catastrophic histories are unique, they have far-reaching and at times painfully urgent implications. The fact remains, however, that in that hauntingly beautiful setting in Berlin, where I had come, against considerable odds, to feel comfortable, and where I withdrew from personal responsibilities in order to make art capturing hard truths, I had failed to read the landscape. Possessing an ancestral history of violence whose full severity and impact are oftentimes not acknowledged, I had nevertheless, in that moment, failed to see another.

You were born, dearest daughter, in the city of Vancouver, on the unceded traditional territories of the Musqueam, Squamish, and Tsleil-Waututh First Nations. You were born on a winter day of intermittent sun and delicate greys, much like this one today, and you should know that you almost didn't make it. I'm not speaking of "making it" in any historical sense, the way your ancestors managed to negotiate and survive their arrival here or really anywhere on earth at all. I'm speaking in straightforward medical terms. Months before your due date, in what was an unusually bright and warm fall, your mother became very sick. At first it was nausea, and a terribly sharp pain. We consulted a family doctor, who suspected a stomach bug and recommended liquids and rest. For hours, your mother, who always prided herself on being tough, tried to relax on a couch, the lamps turned off against her headache. The pain in her gut grew more intense, building into something barely endurable, even for her—until, just as I was about to rush her to the hospital, she experienced a sudden feeling of release and sank into a heavy sleep. Hours went by, until I realized it was not sleep at all but something like a coma. And so, while I had assumed the worst had passed, my loved one was in fact in gravest danger.

It turned out her appendix had burst, and that every minute she lay on the couch, her condition worsened as the toxins coursed through her body. Even when I took her to the emergency room, her condition went undiagnosed for long hours. The acute discomfort had passed, and the medical staff were reluctant to use X-rays on a pregnant woman. The safer alternative, ultrasound, proved ineffective in diagnosing a ruptured appendix, especially in an abdomen distorted by pregnancy. Eventually, a lengthy and very delicate operation was performed (the surgeon afterwards saying, "I never want to do something like that again"), and your mother pulled through, although the recovery was complex. A recurring infection caused sweats and fever spikes, and we made stressful dashes to the hospital for emergency surgery both before and after you were born. Even when her temperature was normal, your mother was in a lot of pain and had trouble keeping down food, with her rounds of antibiotics wreaking additional havoc on her digestive system. I'm sure my own neurotic care didn't always improve her mood. I hovered over her around the clock, extolling the benefits of protein and calcium, of omega-3 fatty acids, and of my own homemade and thickly nourishing broccoli smoothies, inexplicably untouched on her bedside table.

For the birth itself, your mother had hoped for a mid-wife, but our family physician felt that the event needed to be closely monitored, and so an ob-gyn, a somewhat jokey fellow, was assigned. At an ultrasound appointment late in the pregnancy, we inquired nervously about your small size and low weight. "Well, you're no Swedes, either of you," the doctor laughed, being himself tall and blond and possessing a name I only then realized might be Nordic. On the day your mother went into labour, we committed the classic mistake of rushing too early to the hospital, resulting in a long stay in the maternity ward. Late that evening, the doctor arrived, casually examined your mother, and announced he was going home to bed. I stood nervously by as your mother slugged it out all night. I asked her if she wanted water or food. I wet her lips with cotton swabs, and generally fussed about in a way I knew contributed not one whit to the existential struggle before me. And in the morning, the doctor returned, announcing that he'd slept nicely and asking with practised innocence if everyone else in the room had done the same.

You were born around noon, after an effort that remains to me the hardest and frankly most implausible I've ever witnessed. According to your mother, for a brief moment I lost consciousness at your birth, though this is its own small story and point of dispute. But I do remember crouching beside your mother a bit later as she cradled on her stomach a little creature with wet black hair. I remember explaining to her, repeatedly, in a soft and wavering voice, that it was all right, that we were all all right. That the announced weight of six pounds one ounce was decent, was very fine in fact, all things considered. She nodded, a tired smile on her face. "We're no Swedes," she reminded me.

———

We had met, your mother and I, years before, when we were each working on our doctorates. I spotted her wearing blue pyjama pants, a look that you might describe as rather granola, West Coast girl that you are. I suppose I was no better off, fashionably speaking. I suffered from the rather flawed assumption that if you were doing graduate studies in English literature, you needed to dress up. We had each found ourselves specializing in Canadian and "postcolonial" literatures at an infamously

72

ugly university campus, and often in windowless classrooms with buzzing overhead lights where entombed bodies of dead flies vibrated. Sitting across from me for my first class in this auspicious setting was, I remember, your mother, wearing an expression I found difficult to read, although perhaps I was wearing it myself. ("What are you looking at?" "What are *you* looking at?") A bit later into the semester, the two of us found ourselves embroiled in a heated classroom discussion. I can't for the life of me remember the subject of the argument, which probably tells you how important it was. But I do remember how your mother and I each dug in, insisting in increasingly excited terms that our perspectives had not been adequately embraced, our thoughts not yet fully clarified and made known, our feelings insufficiently impressed upon the other. Our fellow students exchanged glances. The professor dryly suggested that perhaps the issue might best be resolved sometime after her class.

I know very well that the love between parents is complex, and not always an easy thing for a child to reflect upon. But you should know that the love I have for your mother is a very real one and that it arose out of a shared passion for broadening, through reading, the cultural and geographic boundaries of what we each knew. This shared passion sustains our relationship, despite what are some rather stark differences in our backgrounds and upbringings.

I remember, for instance, the first time your mother took me to the place you now know, from annual summer vacations, as "the lake." The occasion for this visit was the ninetieth birthday party of her grandfather, your great-grandfather, who was then one of the few surviving naval officers from the Second World War, an accomplished sailor and businessman, as well as a direct descendant of Sir William Mackenzie, a man who made and eventually lost fortunes as one of the railway kings of Canada. I remember that first long drive from Toronto northward into the mythical realm of cottage country, leaving far behind all that was familiar, my eyes riveted upon the blasted rock of the Canadian Shield. Eventually we turned onto a country road, and then a driveway leading a full kilometre into the woods before reaching a clearing revealing a tennis court and a large main cottage, and behind this an expansive back lawn sheltered by mature trees and leading down to a lake with a dock and sailboat. The back lawn is usually a peaceful place, where you can sit taking in the water and green and also a stone fence laid through some rare and beautiful Scottish artisanship. But for the celebration of your great-grandfather's birthday, over a hundred people had been invited, and they were dressed up in their spring finery, and the vast lawn was spread with decorated tables generously piled with food and drink.

From the very beginning of my life with your mother, I have been warmly treated by the families of both your mother's parents. But the day of the party was my first real encounter with a particular Canada made up of business executives, directors of institutions, and arts patrons. I was perhaps the solitary visible minority in the group, and while your relatives are well-travelled, cosmopolitan people who often imagine themselves as not seeing colour, certain guests were a bit less tactful. I was asked several polite and perhaps understandable questions about my relationship to the family. After a couple of rounds of drinks, further polite inquiries were made about my background. One individual, fully into the punch, offered me a complimentary assessment of my racial ancestry. Another guest spontaneously told me stories of his visit to the Caribbean, evoking the pleasantness of the weather, the friendliness of the inhabitants and the happy simplicity of their lives. I received a self-congratulatory discourse on ethnic "tolerance," and on the virtues of our nation as distinct from our neighbour to the south, where there is such distressing tension and violence—"but, of course, more coloureds . . ." When your mother caught up with me, she read my eyes and suggested we should go. "And miss all the fun?" I asked.

What I was most worried about upon that first visit to the lake was my scheduled lunch with your mother's grandparents. It was one thing to encounter such partiers in the outdoors when I could readily excuse myself to gobble up an hors d'oeuvre or down a gin and tonic or visit a bathroom for the sake of both my bladder and my mental wellness. It was quite another to be trapped at a table with two ninety-year-olds who were already adults when segregation of races was not only hard custom but actual law in parts of Canada. And so I braced for more one-sided conversations about ancestry and virtuous "tolerance." But when I was seated beside your great-grandmother, she simply asked, "What are you reading?"

In subsequent visits to the lake, she and I developed a warm relationship built largely around reading. And in time, I came to see the lake in somewhat different terms than I had originally. I learned of a desire to respect summer-home traditions, as well as the natural sur-roundings. Ostentation, as I had witnessed at that very exceptional party, was largely frowned upon. In the main cottage, there was a deliberate absence of many modern household appliances. There was no dishwasher, for example. We were all, guests included, expected to pitch in with cleaning. Drinking water needed to be lugged up from a nearby well, and absolutely no motor-ized water vehicles of any sort were allowed near the dock. All boats needed to be paddled or sailed with an earned demonstration of skill. I learned also that your great-grandmother herself had come from an Anglican family but had married a Catholic man against the not insignificant objections of both family and society. I came to see that she too, in her own way, had journeyed beyond what others expected of her.

I understand that the lake is the site of many of your best summer memories. I know that as guests we are treated very well there, and that you are loved by members of your family who ultimately hail from Sir William Mackenzie, a man who most definitely would never have imagined you as a descendant. Since your birth, especially, I've wanted to believe that people of many backgrounds can find points of commonality in a world of hardened divisions, precious moments of recognition and intimacy across differences, and so begin the necessarily hard work of authentically seeing and hearing one another. Of course, I want to believe that reading and discussing books can play a part in this. But I also want to avoid imagining easy answers to the intricacies of the world, or being blind to persistent hierarchies of power. I want to understand the unspoken sources of wealth, and our often-unacknowledged implication in history. Today, I am someone who can find himself in contexts unfamiliar to many people of my background. But I am also someone who cannot allow such inclusion to blind me to deeper truths.

Among the earlier generation of Canadian poets your mother and I studied together was E.J. Pratt, who wrote an epic poem entitled "Towards the Last Spike," which celebrates in grand, heroic terms the building of the national railway, the very enterprise your distant ancestor profited from. But Pratt's poem does not mention what your mother has pointed out to me—that railway enterprises functioned like weapons against Indigenous peoples, cutting through ancestral lands, violating treaties, and decimating the ecosystems that Indigenous peoples relied upon. Pratt's poem likewise does not mention the indentured Asian workers, sometimes derogatorily called coolies, many of whom died violently when blasting tunnels for the railways, and others both directly and systemically denied citizenship. Such facts are for everyone to learn and remember, and certainly no less for you, being the extremely unlikely descendant of a railway king, but also of Asian coolies, just of a different oceanic journey and of a different bitter and anonymous toil.

You are a complex girl, my daughter. For some of my friends back east, your preferences for sushi and skiing and jackets of functional Gore-Tex instantly identify you as a "Vancouverite." Your mother once, much to my dismay, pronounced you a "camper." And for a short while, you yourself liked the term "tomboy," with its promised alternative to the categories of "girl" and "boy." For some of my relatives, you are Black; for others you are Indian. And as a girl of African, South Asian, and European heritage, some may consider you still another identity, that of being "mixed." Sometimes there is unfair privilege in being mixed, and of thereby avoiding certain degrees of prejudice simply because you might be lighter skinned than other Black or South Asian girls. Other times, there is a foolish denigration associated with being mixed. Of course, as you prove abundantly, there is beauty in being mixed; and I have heard some well-wishing folk proclaim people like you the happy future for humankind, imagining that racial prejudice will come to an end when everyone, through countless inter-mixings, achieves the same features and tone of brown. Forgive me, dearest one, but I don't share this hope. The future I yearn for is not one in which we will all be clothed in sameness, but one in which we will finally learn to both read and respectfully discuss our differences.

And you are a Canadian too, an identity that contains a specific story, promotes specific benefits and ideals, as well as specific illusions and blindnesses. Not so long ago in Canada's history, a girl like you might very well have been denied citizenship, security, and belonging. As your father, I wonder about the extent to which you can now genuinely envision a just future for yourself here. My question is far from unique in the world today, and it links you to young visible minorities in the U.S. and Britain, Australia and Germany, and many other countries.

I remember the moment you became, before my eyes, a Canadian: it was in 2010, when Vancouver hosted the Winter Olympics. You were six and absolutely enthralled by the Games, which we enjoyed on television since tickets were difficult to come by. I watched you watching the pageantry of flags, commercials showing perseverance and the support of families, and the joyful weeping that accompanied the playing of anthems during medal presentations. Your eyelashes were touched with blue from the television screen, your skin that shade midway between the brown of my own and the pink (as you once called it) of your mother's. We were experiencing the wireless technology of nationalism, and I wondered about how we were being manipulated by commercial forces intent on selling furry mascots and official memorabilia and, perhaps, an unconscious acquiescence to questionable civic and national priorities. But I also wondered at the possibilities a six-year-old girl might see for herself in the apparent celebration of peaceful collectivity, human perseverance, and the sheer raw energy of our bodies. Between events, and especially when bedtime threatened, you urgently invented new sports for our living room: the straight-armed and blindfolded pillow toss, the flying couch-propelled bum-bounce. Each time you (inevitably) won an event, you would proudly declare yourself "the Canadian," and, standing on the podium of the couch, belt out the national anthem, before springing towards me for a congratulatory hug.

★

When the men's hockey team won and Canada broke the world record for number of gold medals awarded at a Winter Olympics, you could barely contain your excitement. It was a day of brilliant sunlight, when from our Fairview Slopes neighbourhood the city of Vancouver stood like pale glass before the metallic blues of the northern mountains, and your mother suggested that we should all go outside. We walked the few short minutes from our home to Granville Island, which, of course, is not really an island but a small peninsular mass of land where as a family we have spent so much time at the waterpark and the arts studios and the community centre, and even the somewhat overpriced grocery stores. In 2010, Granville Island was also the home of the Emily Carr University of Art and Design, and I often wrote in its library. Granville Island is also one of the busiest tourist sites in Canada, with streams of visitors taking in the buskers, some buying souvenirs of wild salmon in sterilized vac-packs and syrup in maple-leaf-shaped bottles. On that day when Canada won gold, there were crowds of people milling about the special tents and pavilions celebrating the nations of the world. The massive video screens projected photos of the host city and country, the electric blues of glacial lakes and the shimmering ocean, the deepest greens of the forests. And these same images were replicated on postcards and official merchandise for sale in shops and special vending facilities, a perfect circuit of land and commerce. It was beautiful and unreal, palpable and digitally modified, the way cities and nations very often are.

As we walked, I felt deep gratitude for the warmth of your hand, and for the safety and security we could together enjoy with your mother and brother and the people around us. Although I need to admit I also felt something else, a certain familiar unease, a haunting sense of something missed. Growing up, I understood little about Indigenous peoples. I remember once accidentally learning, from a library book, of a nearby burial site, a hill that marked a presence but also suggested that Indigenous peoples were of the past. I could not then recognize the enduring life around me of the Wendat and the Anishinabek, of the Haudenosaunee Confederacy and the Mississaugas of Scugog Island, of the Hiawatha and the Alderville First Nations and the Métis Nation. I had no knowledge of wampum belts or the historical agreements through which settlers and Indigenous peoples had agreed in good faith to share the resources of the land. Years later, having moved to Vancouver, I quickly learned that I was on the unceded traditional territories of the Musqueam, Squamish, and Tsleil-Waututh First Nations, unceded because the lands had never been voluntarily surrendered. But I didn't immediately understand the specific history of our neighbourhood, especially of Granville Island. This area was always known as Snauq, a place that for many Indigenous peoples functioned as a kind of supermarket, rich with berries and vegetables and seafood. There was a settlement of Indigenous peoples there too, despite the heavy pollution caused by settlers' mills, hotels, and shantytowns, each pumping unsustainable amounts of untreated sewage and waste into the waters of False Creek. And if the cleaning up of False Creek was positive, Granville Island as we know it today was established after the inhabitants of the Indigenous village were forced onto barges to watch as their homes were burned to the ground.

I've learned these hard truths about our neighbourhood because I believe that my ancestors' stories of displacement and vulnerability relate me, inevitably, to similar stories, however implicated I may be in them. Your mother has taught me about Snauq in particular. But I have learned most of all from the raised voices of Indigenous peoples themselves. You are of the first generation of non-Indigenous peoples who have the opportunity to learn the history of Canada's residential schools, and the efforts of our rulers, beginning with our very first prime minister, to arrange for the abduction of Indigenous children from their families and communities for the express purpose of destroying the bond between parent and child. I cannot truly understand the sorrow and echoing violence of the residential schools, or the profundity of the cultural and spiritual resurgence through which Indigenous peoples have reasserted their values and bonds with one another. But I can glimpse, through the lens of my own experience, how a parent or grandparent, encouraged to remain silent and feel ashamed of themselves, may nevertheless find the strength to voice directly to a child a truer story of ancestry, and, in the closeness of voice and breath and chosen language, pass on a legacy of sorrow and power and luminous specificity that honours the past and reveals to the listener a livable future.

Your own ancestral story is also one of luminous specificity. The story I have tried to share with you is of people who were violently exploited and never offered the illusion of automatic belonging here, but who have survived all the same, and have come to sing and love profoundly and to contribute immeasurably to the very nations that have failed to see them. It is a story that relates, in complex ways, to the struggles of Indigenous peoples throughout the world, and also to the desperate migrations of denigrated and "undesirable" peoples, past and present. It is a story that is unashamedly about Black people and South Asian labourers; and it is a story that, precisely thereby, affirms a broader humanity. I offer these words to you with conviction and sincerity, for as your parent I have no right to be otherwise. And yet I also say this with humility, for I know, ultimately, that you will have to find your own answers.

Please know, dearest daughter, that I believe in the experiences you voice and the answers you will find. I believe in your gifts of sight and imagination. I believe, especially, in what you showed me on that bright day as we walked on Granville Island. How, in the midst of the celebration around you, you spotted the homeless woman who sits day after day on the park bench. You noticed her, a human being with a will and a story of her own, and no celebration could distract you from her need.

The rains of winter, the many grey, wet mornings, are here again. During breakfast preparations, the news on the kitchen radio is of the far right in Europe, of the revelation of endemic cultures of sexual harassment and assault, of a ban on transsexuals in the U.S. military, and of nearing the point of no return in global climate change. It was a year ago, out of our shared anxieties about a dawning era of politics, that I first felt the need to write to you, and it is not clear to me just how much has changed. But we do, as a family, have different routines. You have started at a high school that is quite far away, and some days, you bike a good forty minutes in the dark and cold and rain to get there. This is a feat that gains you no sympathy from your tough-girl mother.

And you are tough too, and will insist that you don't need help. But sometimes, when it is especially cold and dark, the rain heavy and icy, I will casually offer you a drive, and, just as casually, you will accept.

There is a distance growing between us, in part the result of the inevitable tensions of growing up. Recently, I tried to impress you by using the word "extra" to describe one of my friends, and you averted your eyes and whispered, "Please stop." Every day you are becoming more yourself. Just a short while ago, we watched you perform in a school play. We were seated in an auditorium with encouraging keeners in front and whooping troublemakers in the back. You walked onto the stage wearing your pink hoodie, but in some ways that was all of you that I recognized. The play was a sweetly silly number about two high school students whose parents wish them to find a date for the prom, even though they don't want to go, and they cycle through the roster of weirdo dates before finding each other. It was amusing, and not very sophisticated, and so why did it affect me so much? Because you were amazing, standing there in front of the audience. Reciting lines that were tired, you somehow found room for complexity, and for your own beautiful self. On the drive this morning, I try, fumblingly, to tell you how struck I was by your beauty, but you shrug impatiently and look outside at the streets floating by.

You are complex. There is your sadness, and there is your wildness. There are the mysteries of your joy—the way you allow chocolate to melt in your fingers while eating it; the little dance you do before pressing an elevator button. There is your silence too, on display today during the car ride, the radio off, nothing but the squeak of the wipers and the patter of rain. In this silence we have arrived at your school, and I pull over and shift into park, but you do not move. You sit still and stare through the windshield. Are you tired? Are you a teenager bored with the prospect of yet another school day? Or is there something you want to say to me about yourself, about the world? "Hey," I ask softly, and you smile and shake your head and open the door, hurry away without looking back.

At the moment of your birth, they say I lost consciousness. They say this because, just before the doctor passed you to your mother, he held you up and asked me a simple question to answer for the room: "Boy or girl?" But I didn't respond. I was caught by your eyes peering back at me unblinking, liquid dark, unfathomable.

People talk about the wonder of first seeing a newborn, of an indescribable moment of joy. And although you have brought endless joy and love into my life, I need to admit that I didn't then feel these things. I felt instead pure fear. I felt the sudden amplification of every doubt I'd ever experienced, every vulnerability. I felt helpless, entirely unable to protect life and imagine freedom. I wasn't ready. I might never be.

You were so small. You weren't crying. Weren't you supposed to be crying? Would you announce yourself? "Boy or girl?" the doctor had asked me. Now you speak your own truths and you will continue to find the scripts that honour your body and experience and history, each of the scripts a gift, and none of them fully adequate to the holy force of you.

But in that moment, you were just a wet little thing with staring eyes. Achingly human. And in that moment, I did the only thing a father could do. I held you and listened.

ACKNOWLEDGEMENTS

Dearest daughter, first and foremost, for your faith and inspiring feedback on this book. Dearest son for your poetry. Dearest Sophie for your love and insight. Martha Kanya-Forstner for your editorial brilliance. Jackie Kaiser for your wise guidance. Phanuel Antwi, Dionne Brand, Mark Chariandy, Kyo Maclear, Sophie McCall, Leslie Sanders, and Christina Sharpe, for your crucial feedback on full drafts. Alicia Elliott, Whitney French, Hiromi Goto, Carrianne Leung, Canisia Lubrin, Minelle Mahtani, Emily Pohl-Weary, Cason Sharpe, Anne Stone, and Jenny Heijun Wills for your crucial feedback on the first chapter. Zetta Elliott for your courageous writing. Geneviève Hill, Lawrence Hill, Abdi Osman, and Rinaldo Walcott for your warm advice. Maximillian Arambulo, Jared Bland, Kristin Cochrane, Marion Garner, Kimberlee Hesas, Ann Jansen, Joe Lee, Terri Nimmo, and all others at PRH Canada for your hard work and support. Carolyn Forde and Meg Wheeler for your advocacy. Alexa von Hirschberg and Callie Garnett for your ongoing interest in my work. My parents, grandparents, and all others before me, for the gifts of life and family.

David Chariandy grew up in Toronto and lives and teaches in Vancouver. His debut novel, *Soucouyant*, was nominated for nearly every major literary prize in Canada. It was shortlisted for the Governor General's Literary Award, won a Gold Independent Publisher Award for Best Novel and was longlisted for the Scotiabank Giller Prize. *Brother*, his second novel, was longlisted for the Scotiabank Giller Prize and won the Rogers Writers' Trust Fiction Prize. This is his first work of non-fiction.

3|19